To

_____

From

_____

Date

_____

My Little Book about Jesus

© 2005 Christian Art Gifts, RSA
        Christian Art Gifts Inc., IL, USA

Compiled by Lynette Douglas
Designed by Christian Art Gifts

Printed in China

ISBN 1-86920-541-3

06 07 08 09 10 11 12 13 14 – 10 9 8 7 6 5 4

My LITTLE BOOK about JESUS

✝ christian
art gifts

CONTENTS

JESUS

Jesus ('dʒiːzəs) *n* 1 Also called: **Jesus Christ, Jesus of Nazareth.** ?4 B.C. – ?29 A.D., founder of Christianity, born in Bethlehem and brought up in Nazareth as a Jew. He is believed by Christians to be the Son of God and to have been miraculously conceived by the Virgin Mary. After the Last Supper with his disciples, he was betrayed by Judas and crucified. Christians believe that he rose from his tomb after three days, appeared to his disciples several times, and ascended to Heaven after 40 days.

Collins Dictionary

"She will give birth to a son, and you are to give him the name Jesus, because he will save his people from their sins."

~ Matthew 1:21 ~

Introduction

The angel Gabriel told Mary and Joseph to call Mary's baby Jesus, because He was destined to save people from their sins.

The name of Jesus has become the sweetest most loved and most revered name on earth. Yet the Bible gives a variety of other names and titles to Jesus, each of which reveals something of His great love for us, and something more of His glory and majesty.

This little book presents some of the best-loved names of Jesus together with Scripture verses that focus on His character.

May it deepen your relationship with your Savior, Jesus Christ, who has a name that is above all names.

Jesus

Therefore God exalted him
to the highest place and gave
him the name that is above
every name, that at the name
of Jesus every knee should bow,
in heaven and on earth
and under the earth.

~ Philippians 2:9-10 ~

Jesus

The name *Jesus* is the Aramaic form of Joshua. It means "The Lord saves". That is why the angel Gabriel told Joseph to give Him the name of Jesus. He came to earth to save us from our sins. He came to be fully man and fully God – perfectly combining deity with humanity.

His earthly life, death and resurrection profoundly affected the history of the world.

His name has become synonymous with all that is lovely, all that is perfect and all that is wonderful. It is the name that soothes our fears, ignites our hope, and inspires our love.

No other name in all the world has such richness, sweetness, depth and passion in it.

From His Word

If you confess with your mouth, "Jesus is Lord," and believe in your heart that God raised him from the dead, you will be saved.

Romans 10:9

Then Jesus came to them and said, "All authority in heaven and on earth has been given to me. Therefore go and make disciples of all nations, baptizing them in the name of the Father and of the Son and of the Holy Spirit."

Matthew 28:18-19

Salvation is found in no one else, for there is no other name under heaven given to men by which we must be saved.

Acts 4:12

His son who through the Spirit of holiness was declared with power to be the Son of God by his resurrection from the dead: Jesus Christ our Lord.

Romans 1:4

Jesus

Jesus Christ is the same yesterday and today and forever.

Hebrews 13:8

By faith in the name of Jesus, this man whom you see and know was made strong. It is Jesus' name and the faith that comes through him that has given this complete healing to him, as you can all see.

Acts 3:16

How sweet the name of Jesus sounds
In a believer's ear!
It soothes his sorrows, heals his wounds,
And drives away his fear.

John Newton

CHRIST

Simon Peter answered,
"You are the Christ,
the Son of the living God."
~ Matthew 16:16 ~

Christist

The Greek word *Christ*, and its Hebrew equivalent *Messiah*, both mean anointed.

The Old Testament promised and prophesied that God would send His anointed One to fulfill the promises of deliverance and usher in a new state of divine blessing. In Old Testament times, kings and priests were anointed with a special oil to confirm their calling from God to fulfill the office to which they had been appointed. They were set aside to do the work of God.

The New Testament recognizes Jesus as "The Anointed One" – the fulfillment of all the types and shadows in the Old Testament. He was sent by God, endued with power from on high, to fulfill the promises of God for mankind.

From His Word

Again the high priest asked him, "Are you the Christ, the Son of the Blessed One?" "I am," said Jesus. "And you will see the Son of Man sitting at the right hand of the Mighty One and coming on the clouds of heaven."

Mark 14:61-62

The first thing Andrew did was to find his brother Simon and tell him, "We have found the Messiah" (that is, the Christ). And he brought him to Jesus.

John 1:41-42

"Therefore let all Israel be assured of this: God has made this Jesus, whom you crucified, both Lord and Christ."

Acts 2:36

For this very reason, Christ died and returned to life so that he might be the Lord of both the dead and the living.

Romans 14:9

Christit

Day after day, in the temple courts and from house to house, they never stopped teaching and proclaiming the good news that Jesus is the Christ.

Acts 5:42

Today in the town of David a Savior has been born to you; he is Christ the Lord.

Luke 2:11

Everyone who believes that Jesus is the Christ is born of God, and everyone who loves the father loves his child as well.

1 John 5:1

> I have a great need for Christ; I have a great Christ for my need.
>
> C. H. Spurgeon

SAVIOR

To the only God
our Savior be glory, majesty,
power and authority,
through Jesus Christ our Lord,
before all ages, now
and forevermore! Amen.

~ Jude 25 ~

Savior

When Adam and Eve sinned by disobeying God, God issued a promise that He would save humankind from sin. The Bible tells the story of how that promise was kept.

The culmination of the promise came when Jesus Christ was born on earth, fully God and fully man, to die for us as the perfect sacrifice that would give us eternal life.

All those who look to Him for salvation, who believe that He is the Savior of the world, receive forgiveness for their sins. Their slates are wiped clean and they receive new life in Him. What a Savior!

From His Word

He was pierced for our transgressions, he was crushed for our iniquities; the punishment that brought us peace was upon him, and by his wounds we are healed.

Isaiah 53:5

She will give birth to a son, and you are to give him the name Jesus, because he will save his people from their sins.

Matthew 1:21

"For God so loved the world that he gave his one and only Son, that whoever believes in him shall not perish but have eternal life. For God did not send his Son into the world to condemn the world, but to save the world through him."

John 3:16-17

Grow in the grace and knowledge of our Lord and Savior Jesus Christ. To him be glory both now and forever! Amen.

2 Peter 3:18

Savior

We wait for the blessed hope – the glorious appearing of our great God and Savior, Jesus Christ, who gave himself for us to redeem us from all wickedness and to purify for himself a people that are his very own, eager to do what is good.

Titus 2:13-14

He then brought them out and asked, "Sirs, what must I do to be saved?" They replied, "Believe in the Lord Jesus, and you will be saved. You and your household."

Acts 16:30-31

One drop of Christ's blood is worth more than heaven and earth.

Martin Luther

Lord

At the name of Jesus every knee
should bow, in heaven and on
earth and under the earth, and every
tongue confess that Jesus Christ is
Lord, to the glory of God the Father.

~ Philippians 2:10-11 ~

Lord

Christ is referred to as Lord more than 500 times in the New Testament. Because He is the Lord of lords He has the authority to rule over all of creation, in your heart and in your life.

When Jesus told the Jews that He is I AM, He used the Hebrew word for Jehovah, which means "Lord". It signifies the eternal nature of God and His supremacy and sovereignty over heaven and earth. He is the eternally self-existent One who does not change.

What a comfort it is to yield to the lordship of Christ, because as we do He comes to save, help, deliver, redeem and bless us. He keeps His covenant with us.

From His Word

"See, I will send my messenger, who will prepare the way before me. Then suddenly the Lord you are seeking will come to his temple; the messenger of the covenant, whom you desire, will come," says the LORD Almighty.

Malachi 3:1

"Not everyone who says to me, 'Lord, Lord,' will enter the kingdom of heaven, but only he who does the will of my Father who is in heaven."

Matthew 7:21

Simon Peter answered him, "Lord, to whom shall we go? You have the words of eternal life. We believe and know that you are the Holy One of God."

John 6:68-69

For if you do these things, you will never fall, and you will receive a rich welcome into the eternal kingdom of our Lord and Savior Jesus Christ.

2 Peter 1:10-11

Lord

Each of the four living creatures had six wings and was covered with eyes all around, even under his wings. Day and night they never stop saying: "Holy, holy, holy is the Lord God Almighty, who was, and is, and is to come."

Revelation 4:8

"Great and marvelous are your deeds, Lord God Almighty. Just and true are your ways, King of the ages. Who will not fear you, O Lord, and bring glory to your name? For you alone are holy. All nations will come and worship before you, for your righteous acts have been revealed."

Revelation 15:3-4

There is not an inch of any sphere of life over which Jesus Christ does not say, "Mine!"

Abraham Kuyper

SON OF GOD

If anyone acknowledges that
Jesus is the Son of God,
God lives in him and he in God.

~ 1 John 4:15 ~

Son of God

Jesus is the Son of God, the Second Person of the Trinity. He is fully God and stands in a unique relationship with the Father.

All the attributes and authority that God has are found in Jesus. He is equal with God in power and glory and is worthy of all honor, praise and worship.

Jesus came to earth as both Man and God to show us the nature of God and to lead us back to the Father.

Jesus said that those who have seen Him have seen the Father. When we look at the life of Jesus, we see the compassion, grace and love the Father has for us.

From His Word

The angel answered, "The Holy Spirit will come upon you, and the power of the Most High will overshadow you. So the holy one to be born will be called the Son of God."

Luke 1:35

And this is the testimony: God has given us eternal life, and this life is in his Son. He who has the Son has life; he who does not have the Son of God does not have life.

1 John 5:11-12

I have been crucified with Christ and I no longer live, but Christ lives in me. The life I live in the body, I live by faith in the Son of God, who loved me and gave himself for me.

Galatians 2:20

"For just as the Father raises the dead and gives them life, even so the Son gives life to whom he is pleased to give it."

John 5:21

Son of God

And a voice from heaven said, "This is my Son, whom I love; with him I am well pleased."

Matthew 3:17

After Jesus said this, he looked toward heaven and prayed: "Father, the time has come. Glorify your Son, that your Son may glorify you."

John 17:1

Then Nathanael declared, "Rabbi, you are the Son of God; you are the King of Israel."

John 1:49

> If ever man was God or God man, Jesus Christ was both.
>
> Lord Byron

Immanuel

The virgin will be with child
and will give birth to a son,
and they will call him Immanuel
which means, "God with us."

~ Matthew 1:23 ~

Immanuel

Immanuel – God with us! Of all the designations of Jesus, this one holds the deepest comfort.

God did not remain in heaven, removed from our hardships and difficulties in the world. He came to earth to be with us and to show how deeply and sincerely He loves us.

Jesus promised that He would always be with us – that He would never leave us or forsake us. So no matter what difficulties we face in life, we know that our God cares for us, and is very near to help us in our time of need.

From His Word

Therefore the LORD himself will give you a sign: The virgin will be with child and will give birth to a son, and will call him Immanuel.

Isaiah 7:14

But when the time had fully come, God sent his Son, born of a woman, born under law, to redeem those under law, that we might receive the full rights of sons.

Galatians 4:4-5

The Word became flesh and made his dwelling among us. We have seen his glory, the glory of the One and Only, who came from the Father, full of grace and truth.

John 1:14

The mystery of godliness is great: He appeared in a body, was vindicated by the Spirit, was seen by angels, was preached among the nations, was believed on in the world, was taken up in glory.

1 Timothy 3:16

Immanuel

This is how God showed his love among us: He sent his one and only Son into the world that we might live through him.

1 John 4:9

Christ Jesus: Who, being in very nature God, did not consider equality with God something to be grasped, but made himself nothing, taking the very nature of a servant ... he humbled himself and became obedient to death – even death on a cross!

Philippians 2:5-8

> Immanuel, God with us in our nature, in our sorrow, in our lifework, in our punishment, in our grave, and now with us, or rather we with Him, in resurrection, ascension, triumph, and Second Advent splendor.
>
> C. H. Spurgeon

ALPHA AND OMEGA

"I am the Alpha and the Omega,"
says the Lord God,
"Who is, and who was, and
who is to come, the Almighty."
~ Revelation 1:8 ~

Alpha and Omega

Jesus is eternal. Before time began, He already existed, and He will never cease to exist.

He is the Alpha and all things have their origin in Him. He created all there is, and He alone has absolute authority over creation. He is the only one who can make all things new.

As the Omega, the last, He alone knows the future and will finally bring to fruition all things to the glory of God. He is in control of the future and knows the end from the beginning.

When the world comes to an end and He sits on the throne judging all mankind, He will banish death, punish the wicked and reward those who love and obey Him.

From His Word:

Now to the King eternal, immortal, invisible, the only God, be honor and glory for ever and ever. Amen.

1 Timothy 1:17

Before the mountains were born or you brought forth the earth and the world, from everlasting to everlasting you are God.

Psalm 90:2

Grace and peace to you from him who is, and who was, and who is to come, and from the seven spirits before his throne, and from Jesus Christ, who is the faithful witness, the firstborn from the dead, and the ruler of the kings of the earth.

Revelation 1:4-5

The LORD brought me forth as the first of his works, before his deeds of old; I was appointed from eternity, from the beginning, before the world began.

Proverbs 8:22-23

Alpha and Omega

He is before all things, and in him all things hold together.

Colossians 1:17

Can you imagine the number of words it took to write a thirty-volume set of the Encyclopedia Britannica? It must be an awesome number. More amazing is that only twenty-six different letters were used. The authors did not go outside the alphabet to assemble that massive collection of knowledge. It provided for them everything they needed for this task.

Jesus Christ called Himself the Alpha and Omega, and we do not have to go outside of Him for anything we need. He is God's "everything" – for all situations.

Unknown

Mighty God

For to us a child is born, to us a son
is given, and the government will be
on his shoulders. And he will be called
Wonderful Counselor, Mighty God,
Everlasting Father, Prince of Peace.

~ Isaiah 9:6 ~

Mighty God

Jesus is the Mighty God – in Him resides all power and strength. He is able to do all things.

He is the conquering King who defeats all wickedness.

He is the powerful God who created all things and through whom the universe is held together.

He is the victorious Lord who triumphed over death and Satan.

There is no one like God. No one as powerful. No one as righteous. No one as faithful. No one as true.

In Him we find strength in our hour of weakness, help in our time of need, and peace in the midst of chaos.

From His Word

But about the Son he says, "Your throne, O God, will last for ever and ever, and righteousness will be the scepter of your kingdom."

Hebrews 1:8

This is what the LORD says – Israel's King and Redeemer, the LORD Almighty: I am the first and I am the last; apart from me there is no God.

Isaiah 44:6

But the LORD Almighty will be exalted by his justice, and the holy God will show himself holy by his righteousness.

Isaiah 5:16

O LORD God Almighty, who is like you? You are mighty, O LORD, and your faithfulness surrounds you.

Psalm 89:8

Mighty God

O LORD Almighty, God of Israel, enthroned between the cherubim, you alone are God over all the kingdoms of the earth. You have made heaven and earth.

Isaiah 37:16

I did not see a temple in the city, because the Lord God Almighty and the Lamb are its temple.

Revelation 21:22

"We give thanks to you, Lord God Almighty, the One who is and who was, because you have taken your great power and have begun to reign."

Revelation 11:17

When Jesus is present all is well, and nothing seems difficult.

Thomas á Kempis

Prince of Peace

"Peace I leave with you;
my peace I give you.
I do not give to you
as the world gives.
Do not let your hearts be
troubled and do not be afraid."

~ John 14:27 ~

Prince of Peace

The God of Peace gives us the gift of His peace. When Christ came into the world, the angels brought a message of peace.

When He left this world, He told His disciples that He was leaving His peace with them. He came to make the peace of God a reality in our lives.

When He rules and reigns in our hearts and lives, peace will flood our souls.

Jesus, the Prince of Peace, comes to you when you are worried, frightened, stressed or uncertain. He brings you peace that calms your soul, eases your mind and satisfies your heart.

From His Word:

Do not be anxious about anything, but in everything, by prayer and petition, with thanksgiving, present your requests to God. And the peace of God, which transcends all understanding, will guard your hearts and your minds in Christ Jesus.

Philippians 4:6-7

You will keep in perfect peace him whose mind is steadfast, because he trusts in you.

Isaiah 26:3

Jesus came and stood among them and said, "Peace be with you!"

John 20:19

For he himself is our peace, who has made the two one and has destroyed the barrier, the dividing wall of hostility.

Ephesians 2:14

Prince of Peace

"I have told you these things, so that in me you may have peace. In this world you will have trouble. But take heart! I have overcome the world."

John 16:33

Now may the Lord of peace himself give you peace at all times and in every way. The Lord be with all of you.

2 Thessalonians 3:16

Christ alone can bring lasting peace – peace with God – peace among men and nations – and peace within our hearts.

Billy Graham

WONDERFUL COUNSELOR

This also comes from
the LORD of hosts,
who is wonderful in counsel
and excellent in guidance.

~ Isaiah 28:29, NKJV ~

Wonderful Counselor

There are many people who try to give us advice about the way we should live our lives.

But only Christ gives counsel that is consistently reliable and will undoubtedly lead to a life of abundance.

He came to show us the way to live in obedience to God. He leads us along the paths of righteousness that lead to life.

He is always near us to guide us through His Holy Spirit. If we seek His face and ask for wisdom in every situation we face, we will walk with confidence even through the darkest valleys.

From His Word

My dear children, I write this to you so that you will not sin. But if anybody does sin, we have one who speaks to the Father in our defense – Jesus Christ, the Righteous One.

1 John 2:1

I will instruct you and teach you in the way you should go; I will counsel you and watch over you. Do not be like the horse or the mule, which have no understanding but must be controlled by bit and bridle or they will not come to you.

Psalm 32:8-9

The LORD foils the plans of the nations; he thwarts the purposes of the peoples. But the plans of the LORD stand firm forever, the purposes of his heart through all generations.

Psalm 33:10-11

"To God belong wisdom and prayer; counsel and understanding are his."

Job 12:13

Wonderful Counselor

I will praise the LORD who counsels me; even at night my heart instructs me.

Psalm 16:7

The counsel of the LORD stands forever, the plans of His heart to all generations.

Psalm 33:11, NKJV

Thus God, determining to show more abundantly to the heirs of promise the immutability of His counsel, confirmed it by an oath.

Hebrews 6:17, NKJV

The truly wise are those whose souls are in Christ.

St. Ambrose

LIGHT OF THE WORLD

When Jesus spoke again
to the people, he said,
"I am the light of the world.
Whoever follows me
will never walk in darkness,
but will have the light of life."

~ John 8:12 ~

Light of the world

Jesus Christ came into this dark world to bring light and life to all people.

He brought the radiance of God's glory into the lives of people who were lost and without hope, groping to find their way through the darkness of immorality, injustice and sin.

He is the light that brings hope and healing to our hearts.

The glory of God was manifested through the works that Christ did and culminated when He defeated darkness once and for all when He rose from the dead. Because He lives, we need not fear darkness or death.

From His Word

Keep this command without spot or blame until the appearing of our Lord Jesus Christ, which God will bring about in his own time – God, the blessed and only Ruler, the King of kings and Lord of lords, who alone is immortal and who lives in unapproachable light, whom no one has seen or can see. To him be honor and might forever. Amen.

1 Timothy 6:14-16

Arise, shine, for your light has come, and the glory of the LORD rises upon you. See, darkness covers the earth and thick darkness is over the peoples, but the LORD rises upon you and his glory appears over you.

Isaiah 60:1-2

The LORD is my light and my salvation – whom shall I fear? The LORD is the stronghold of my life.

Psalm 27:1

Light of the world

In him was life, and that life was the light of men. The light shines in the darkness, but the darkness has not understood it.

John 1:4-5

"The people living in darkness have seen a great light; on those living in the land of the shadow of death a light has dawned."

Matthew 4:16

A glimpse of the glory of God in the face of Jesus Christ causes in the heart a supreme genuine love for God. This is because the divine light shows the excellent loveliness of God's nature.

Jonathan Edwards

THE GOOD SHEPHERD

"I am the good shepherd;
I know my sheep and
my sheep know me –
just as the Father knows me
and I know the Father –
and I lay down my life
for the sheep."

~ John 10:14-15 ~

The Good Shepherd

Jesus is the Good Shepherd who protects His sheep, leading them along the quiet paths of life, refreshing them with still waters. His way is a way of peace and serenity.

We walk in safety when we follow Him because He protects us from all dangers, from all who want to harm us.

He will seek for the one who is lost, and will not rest until the lost lamb is safely back in His fold. His sheep know His voice and follow Him alone.

As we live our lives in His care, we will hear when He warns us of danger, we will know the provisions He supplies and we will be assured of His love.

From His Word

"I am the good shepherd; I know my sheep and my sheep know me – just as the Father knows me and I know the Father – and I lay down my life for the sheep."

John 10:14-15

The LORD is my shepherd, I shall not be in want. He makes me lie down in green pastures, he leads me beside quiet waters, he restores my soul. He guides me in paths of righteousness for his name's sake.

Psalm 23:1-3

He tends his flock like a shepherd: He gathers the lambs in his arms and carries them close to his heart; he gently leads those that have young.

Isaiah 40:11

Know that the LORD is God. It is he who made us, and we are his; we are his people, the sheep of his pasture.

Psalm 100:3

The Good Shepherd

"What do you think? If a man owns a hundred sheep, and one of them wanders away, will he not leave the ninety-nine on the hills and go to look for the one that wandered off?"

Matthew 18:12

For you were like sheep going astray, but now you have returned to the Shepherd and Overseer of your souls.

1 Peter 2:25

The King of love my Shepherd is,
Whose goodness faileth never;
I nothing lack if I am His
And He is mine forever.

Henry Williams Baker

BREAD OF LIFE

Then Jesus declared,
"I am the bread of life.
He who comes to me
will never go hungry,
and he who believes in me
will never be thirsty."

~ John 6:35 ~

Bread of Life

When Jesus called Himself the Bread of Life, He was saying that it was only by partaking of His life that we would have true life.

When we eat the bread of communion we remember that Christ died for us. The bread symbolizes His body that was broken on the cross for us – through which we receive eternal life.

Man does not live on bread alone. Our bodies may be fed, but if our souls are starving we will not experience the fullness of life.

When we believe in Him and partake of the Bread of Life He offers, we will truly live.

From His Word

"Do not work for food that spoils, but for food that endures to eternal life, which the Son of Man will give you. On him God the Father has placed his seal of approval."

John 6:27

Jesus said to them, "I tell you the truth, unless you eat the flesh of the Son of Man and drink his blood, you have no life in you."

John 6:53

For I received from the Lord what I also passed on to you: The Lord Jesus, on the night he was betrayed, took bread, and when he had given thanks, he broke it and said, "This is my body, which is for you; do this in remembrance of me."

1 Corinthians 11:23-24

Jesus answered, "It is written: 'Man does not live on bread alone, but on every word that comes from the mouth of God.'"

Matthew 4:4

Bread of Life

"For the bread of God is he who comes down from heaven and gives life to the world."

John 6:33

While they were eating, Jesus took bread, gave thanks and broke it, and gave it to his disciples, saying, "Take and eat; this is my body."

Matthew 26:26

"But here is the bread that comes down from heaven, which a man may eat and not die."

John 6:50

The name of Jesus is not only light but food. It is oil without which food for the soul is dry, and salt without which it is insipid. It is honey in the mouth, melody in the ear and joy in the heart.

Bernard of Clairvaux

LAMB OF GOD

The next day John saw
Jesus coming toward him and said,
"Look, the Lamb of God, who takes
away the sin of the world!"

~ John 1:29 ~

Lamb of God

God's judgment on sin is death. But God made a way in which a sacrifice of a pure, unblemished lamb could take away our sins.

Jesus is the Lamb of God who, through His blood shed on the cross, washes us clean and makes us holy and presentable to God.

His sacrifice is our salvation. If He had not died in our place, we would all be doomed to destruction. But because of His great love for us, He died so that we can live with Him forever.

Let us praise the Lamb that was slain, because He is worthy of all honor and glory!

From His Word

In a loud voice they sang: "Worthy is the Lamb, who was slain, to receive power and wealth and wisdom and strength and honor and glory and praise!"

Revelation 5:12

Then I heard every creature in heaven and on earth and under the earth and on the sea, and all that is in them, singing: "To him who sits on the throne and to the Lamb be praise and honor and glory and power, for ever and ever!"

Revelation 5:13

We all, like sheep, have gone astray, each of us has turned to his own way; and the Lord has laid on him the iniquity of us all.

Isaiah 53:6

Abraham answered, "God himself will provide the lamb for the burnt offering, my son." And the two of them went on together.

Genesis 22:8

Lamb of God

For you know that it was not with perishable things such as silver or gold that you were redeemed from the empty way of life handed down to you from your forefathers, but with the precious blood of Christ, a lamb without defect.

1 Peter 1:18-19

Get rid of the old yeast that you may be a new batch without yeast – as you really are. For Christ, our Passover lamb, has been sacrificed.

1 Corinthians 5:7

We are told that Christ was killed for us, that His death has washed out our sins, and that by dying He disabled death itself. That is the formula. That is Christianity. That is what has to be believed.

C. S. Lewis

TEACHER

Jesus said to her, "Mary."
She turned toward him
and cried out in Aramaic,
"Rabboni!" (which means Teacher).

~ John 20:16 ~

Teacher

When Mary called Jesus *Rabboni*, a title of respect and honor, she reflected the disciples' attitude toward Him.

He was their Lord and Master, and they acknowledged His authority to teach them about the Kingdom of God. Jesus taught in many ways – through sermons, stories and through the way He lived.

Jesus taught about the grace, love and mercy of God. He instructed His disciples in the ways of obedience to the will of God. His teaching was tempered with love and compassion and reflected the Father's heart.

From His Word

"You call me 'Teacher' and 'Lord,' and rightly so, for that is what I am. Now that I, your Lord and Teacher, have washed your feet, you also should wash one another's feet."

John 13:13-14

When Jesus had finished saying these things, the crowds were amazed at his teaching, because he taught as one who had authority, and not as their teachers of the law.

Matthew 7:28-29

"A student is not above his teacher, nor a servant above his master. It is enough for the student to be like his teacher, and the servant like his master."

Matthew 10:24-25

It is written in the Prophets: "They will all be taught by God. Everyone who listens to the Father and learns from him comes to me."

John 6:45

Teacher

To the Jews who had believed him, Jesus said, "If you hold to my teaching, you are really my disciples."

John 8:31

"You have one Teacher, the Christ."

Matthew 23:10

Jesus replied, "If anyone loves me, he will obey my teaching. My Father will love him, and we will come to him and make our home with him."

John 14:23

> The teaching of Christ is more excellent than all the advice of the saints, and he who has His Spirit will find in it a hidden manna.
>
> Thomas á Kempis

THE RESURRECTION
AND THE LIFE

Jesus said to her, "I am
the resurrection and the life.
He who believes in me will live,
even though he dies;
and whoever lives
and believes in me will never die.
Do you believe this?"

~ John 11:25-26 ~

The resurrection and the life

The miracle of the resurrection is the heart of the gospel of Christ. When Jesus triumphed over death and rose again, it became possible for believers to inherit eternal life. He defeated sin and death, and made it possible for us to live forever.

Because Jesus rose from the dead, we become new creations with new life, freed from the curse of sin and death.

Through Jesus' resurrection, we have the assurance that we too will not be defeated by death. We will rise again with a new body that is incorruptible and perfect. Christ gives us life and that more abundantly!

From His Word

With long life will I satisfy him and show him my salvation.

Psalm 91:16

Through him all things were made; without him nothing was made that has been made. In him was life, and that life was the light of men.

John 1:3-4

The life appeared; we have seen it and testify to it, and we proclaim to you the eternal life, which was with the Father and has appeared to us. We proclaim to you what we have seen and heard, so that you also may have fellowship with us. And our fellowship is with the Father and with his Son, Jesus Christ.

1 John 1:2-3

But these are written that you may believe that Jesus is the Christ, the Son of God, and that by believing you may have life in his name.

John 20:31

The resurrection and the life

When Christ, who is your life, appears, then you also will appear with him in glory.

Colossians 3:4

He who has the Son has life; he who does not have the Son of God does not have life.

1 John 5:12

"Because I live, you also will live."

John 14:19

The Lord Jesus came into this world not primarily to say something, not even to be something, but to do something; He came not merely to lead men through His example into a "larger life," but to give life, through His death and resurrection, to those who were dead in trespasses and sins.

J. Gresham Machen

HOLY ONE OF GOD

Simon Peter answered him,
"Lord, to whom shall we go?
You have the words of eternal life.
We believe and know
that you are the Holy One of God."

~ John 6:68-69 ~

Holy One of God

Jesus Christ is fully man and fully God. He has all the characteristics of man, and yet He is without sin. Throughout His life on earth, Christ was separated from sin and dedicated to the glory of God.

Jesus Christ is absolutely pure and so was able to be the perfect sacrifice – without spot or blemish – untainted by the sinful nature of mankind.

That is why He can set us free from sin, and calls us to live a life of perfect holiness, separated from the sin of the world, dedicated to serving the Father.

From His Word

You will not abandon me to the grave, nor will you let your Holy One see decay.

Psalm 16:10

The angel answered, "The Holy Spirit will come upon you, and the power of the Most High will overshadow you. So the holy one to be born will be called the Son of God."

Luke 1:35

This righteousness from God comes through faith in Jesus Christ to all who believe.

Romans 3:22

It is because of him that you are in Christ Jesus, who has become for us wisdom from God – that is, our righteousness, holiness and redemption.

1 Corinthians 1:30

I am the LORD your God; consecrate yourselves and be holy, because I am holy.

Leviticus 11:44

Holy One of God

And they were calling to one another: "Holy, holy, holy is the LORD Almighty; the whole earth is full of his glory."

Isaiah 6:3

Such a high priest meets our need – one who is holy, blameless, pure, set apart from sinners, exalted above the heavens.

Hebrews 7:26

Then he said: "The God of our fathers has chosen you to know his will and to see the Righteous One and to hear words from his mouth."

Acts 22:14

To love Jesus is to love holiness.
David Smithers

SON OF MAN

"The Son of Man
must be delivered
into the hands of sinful men,
be crucified and
on the third day
be raised again."

~ Luke 24:7 ~

Son of man

This was Jesus' favorite description of Himself and it is found more than 80 times in the Gospels. When Jesus used this term, He was reminding us that He, who is God, came and lived on earth as a man so that He could identify with us in every way.

He, the Creator of the universe, became like one of the people He made so that we could know the greatness of God's love for us.

We do not serve a God who has no understanding for our situation. He knows what it is like to live in this world and to be confined by the limitations of time and space.

How wonderful that He loved us so much that He came to live among us to draw us to Himself.

From His Word

"When the Son of Man comes in his glory, and all the angels with him, he will sit on his throne in heavenly glory."

Matthew 25:31

"For the Son of Man is going to come in his Father's glory with his angels, and then he will reward each person according to what he has done."

Matthew 16:27

When Jesus came to the region of Caesarea Philippi, he asked his disciples, "Who do people say the Son of Man is?" "But what about you?" he asked. "Who do you say I am?" Simon Peter answered, "You are the Christ, the Son of the living God."

Matthew 16:13, 16

"No one has ever gone into heaven except the one who came from heaven – the Son of Man."

John 3:13

Son of man

"In my vision at night I looked, and there before me was one like a son of man, coming with the clouds of heaven. He was given authority, glory and sovereign power; all peoples, nations and men of every language worshiped him."

Daniel 7:13-14

I looked, and there before me was a white cloud, and seated on the cloud was one "like a son of man" with a crown of gold on his head and a sharp sickle in his hand.

Revelation 14:14

Christ's humanity is the great hem of the garment through which we can touch His Godhead.

Richard Glover

FAITHFUL FRIEND

"I no longer call you servants,
because a servant does not know
his master's business.
Instead, I have called you friends,
for everything that I learned
from my Father I
have made known to you."

~ John 15:15 ~

Faithful friend

God does not distance Himself from His people. He is not unapproachable. He created us because He delights in our fellowship and He wants to be our friend! He wants to be near us, and He wants us to love Him too.

Jesus is our faithful friend. We will never find anyone more committed to us, more willing for us to succeed, and more able to help us become all that we are capable of being.

As we fellowship with Him, our lives embrace a richness and depth that encourages us to live lives worthy of the servants and friends of the King.

From His Word

"Greater love has no one than this, that he lay down his life for his friends."

John 15:13

"The Son of Man came eating and drinking, and they say, 'Here is a glutton and a drunkard, a friend of tax collectors and sinners.' But wisdom is proved right by her actions."

Matthew 11:19

A man of many companions may come to ruin, but there is a friend who sticks closer than a brother.

Proverbs 18:24

"You are my friends if you do what I command."

John 15:14

Jesus replied, "If anyone loves me, he will obey my teaching. My Father will love him, and we will come to him and make our home with him."

John 14:23

Faithful friend

God, who has called you into fellowship with his
Son Jesus Christ our Lord, is faithful.

1 Corinthians 1:9

Those who obey his commands live in him, and
he in them. And this is how we know that he lives
in us: We know it by the Spirit he gave us.

1 John 3:24

"Here I am! I stand at the door and knock. If
anyone hears my voice and opens the door, I will
come in and eat with him, and he with me."

Revelation 3:20

For however devoted you are to God, you
may be sure that He is immeasurably more
devoted to you.

Meister Eckhart

THE VINE

"I am the vine;
you are the branches.
If a man remains
in me and I in him,
he will bear much fruit;
apart from me
you can do nothing."

~ John 15:5 ~

The Vine

Jesus Christ is the true vine – the only means through which we can produce godly fruit in our lives. As we allow Him to fill us with His life-giving strength, we will begin to bear the fruit of Christ-likeness in our lives.

Our lives will be fragrant and delightful and will bless many who are touched by the presence of Christ in our hearts.

There is no real godliness without the presence of Christ. There is no real and lasting beauty in our lives if God is not the Gardener who prunes and nurtures us.

If we remain in Him our lives will permeate the sweetness of His love, joy, peace, goodness and kindness.

From His Word

Once more a remnant of the house of Judah will take root below and bear fruit above.

2 Kings 19:30

You brought a vine out of Egypt; you drove out the nations and planted it. You cleared the ground for it, and it took root and filled the land. The root your right hand has planted, the son you have raised up for yourself.

Psalm 80:8-9, 15

He grew up before him like a tender shoot, and like a root out of dry ground. He had no beauty or majesty to attract us to him, nothing in his appearance that we should desire him.

Isaiah 53:2

"Remain in me, and I will remain in you. No branch can bear fruit by itself; it must remain in the vine. Neither can you bear fruit unless you remain in me."

John 15:4

The Vine

"You did not choose me, but I chose you and appointed you to go and bear fruit – fruit that will last. Then the Father will give you whatever you ask in my name."

John 15:16

But the fruit of the Spirit is love, joy, peace, patience, kindness, goodness, faithfulness, gentleness and self-control.

Galatians 5:22-23

It is the laden bough that hangs low, and the most fruitful Christian who is the most humble.

Unknown

THE WAY, THE TRUTH AND THE LIFE

Jesus answered, "I am the way
and the truth and the life.
No one comes to the Father
except through me."

~ John 14:6 ~

The way, truth and life

Jesus is all we need to get to heaven. He is the way – not only does He show us the way, but He is also the doorway that leads to eternal life. As we abide in Him and walk with Him, we are walking in the ways that lead to life and a glorious future in heaven.

He is the truth. Everything He says is true. Because we can depend on Him, because He is trustworthy, we can know that the way He shows us is dependable and perfect.

If we follow Him we can be certain of eternal life. In Him life is full, delightful, abundant and prosperous.

From His Word

To the Jews who had believed him, Jesus said, "If you hold to my teaching, you are really my disciples. Then you will know the truth, and the truth will set you free."

John 8:31-32

We know also that the Son of God has come and has given us understanding, so that we may know him who is true. And we are in him who is true – even in his Son Jesus Christ. He is the true God and eternal life.

1 John 5:20

"These are the words of the Amen, the faithful and true witness, the ruler of God's creation."

Revelation 3:14

"I am the gate; whoever enters through me will be saved. He will come in and go out, and find pasture."

John 10:9

The way, truth and life

Show me your ways, O LORD, teach me your paths.

Psalm 25:4

"Enter through the narrow gate. For wide is the gate and broad is the road that leads to destruction, and many enter through it. But small is the gate and narrow the road that leads to life, and only a few find it."

Matthew 7:13-14

Come, my Way, my Truth, my Life:
Such a Way that gives us breath:
Such a Truth as ends all strife:
And such a Life as killeth death.

George Herbert

THE WORD

In the beginning
was the Word,
and the Word was with God,
and the Word was God.

~ John 1:1 ~

The Word

God reveals Himself and His will to people through the Word. Through the Word of God, His sovereign purposes are accomplished in the world. When John began his gospel by declaring that "In the beginning was the Word," he was confirming that God had revealed Himself to us in a new way – in the very person of Jesus Christ, God in the flesh.

Through Jesus we have a clearer understanding of the message of love and salvation that God brings to every person. Christ as the Word constitutes the complete and ultimate divine revelation. Only in and through Jesus does God fully express Himself. Through Jesus, God communicates His thoughts and intentions to us in a language we can understand – a language of the heart.

From His Word

That which was from the beginning, which we have heard, which we have seen with our eyes, which we have looked at and our hands have touched – this we proclaim concerning the Word of life.

1 John 1:1

In the past God spoke to our forefathers through the prophets at many times and in various ways, but in these last days he has spoken to us by his Son, whom he appointed heir of all things, and through whom he made the universe.

Hebrews 1:1-2

His eyes are like blazing fire, and on his head are many crowns. He has a name written on him that no one knows but he himself. He is dressed in a robe dipped in blood, and his name is the Word of God.

Revelation 19:12-13

The Word

Let us fix our eyes on Jesus, the author and perfecter of our faith, who for the joy set before him endured the cross, scorning its shame, and sat down at the right hand of the throne of God.

Hebrews 12:2

In bringing many sons to glory, it was fitting that God, for whom and through whom everything exists, should make the author of their salvation perfect through suffering.

Hebrews 2:10

When Jesus Christ utters a word, He opens His mouth so wide that it embraces all heaven and earth, even though that word be but a whisper.

Martin Luther

HIGH PRIEST

Therefore, since we have
a great high priest who
has gone through the heavens,
Jesus the Son of God,
let us hold firmly
to the faith we profess.

~ Hebrews 4:14 ~

High Priest

In the Old Testament the High Priest represented the nation of Israel before God, asking pardon on their behalf by offering the blood of the sacrificial lamb. But this was an imperfect sacrifice made by an imperfect person.

When Christ died on the cross, He entered the Holy Place in heaven – of which the temple had only been a picture – and presented His own blood as the perfect sacrifice that atoned for all the sins of all people through all time. All we need to do is, by faith, accept that He has done so, and all our sins will be forgiven.

As our High Priest, Christ is constantly interceding before the Father on our behalf. He is our representative in heaven as we are His representatives on earth.

From His Word

We do have such a high priest, who sat down at the right hand of the throne of the Majesty in heaven, and who serves in the sanctuary, the true tabernacle set up by the Lord, not by man.

Hebrews 8:1-2

How much more, then, will the blood of Christ, who through the eternal Spirit offered himself unblemished to God, cleanse our consciences from acts that lead to death, so that we may serve the living God!

Hebrews 9:14

We have this hope as an anchor for the soul, firm and secure. It enters the inner sanctuary behind the curtain, where Jesus, who went before us, has entered on our behalf.

Hebrews 6:19-20

High Priest

Such a high priest meets our need – One who is holy, blameless, pure, set apart from sinners, exalted above the heavens. Unlike the other high priests, he does not need to offer sacrifices day after day, first for his own sins, and then for the sins of the people. He sacrificed for their sins once for all when he offered himself.

Hebrews 7:26-27

Fix your thoughts on Jesus, the apostle and high priest whom we confess.

Hebrews 3:1

When Jesus bowed His head,
And dying took our place,
The veil was rent, a way was found
To that pure home of grace.

John Elias

MORNING STAR

"I, Jesus, have sent
my angel to give you
this testimony for the churches.
I am the Root and
the Offspring of David,
and the bright Morning Star."

~ Revelation 22:16 ~

Morning Star

When Jesus came to live on earth He brought a new dawn – the dawn of a day that will never end and will always be flooded with the light of the radiant presence of God. He brought the light of God's eternal day into the world that was covered by the darkness of sin.

When Jesus rose as the Sun of Righteousness in our midst, He brought with Him health and healing and all that is needed for us to live in the light of God. He revives us, as a man is revived when he sees the sun rising after a long, dark night.

When His light dawns in our lives, we are refreshed and renewed, and we find strength to face each day.

From His Word

But for you who revere my name, the sun of righteousness will rise with healing in its wings. And you will go out and leap like calves released from the stall.

Malachi 4:2

And we have the word of the prophets made more certain, and you will do well to pay attention to it, as to a light shining in a dark place, until the day dawns and the morning star rises in your hearts.

2 Peter 1:19

"Where is the one who has been born king of the Jews? We saw his star in the east and have come to worship him."

Matthew 2:2

In his right hand he held seven stars, and out of his mouth came a sharp double-edged sword. His face was like the sun shining in all its brilliance.

Revelation 1:16

Morning Star

And you, my child, will go on before the Lord to prepare the way for him, to give his people the knowledge of salvation through the forgiveness of their sins, because of the tender mercy of our God, by which the rising sun will come to us from heaven to shine on those living in darkness and in the shadow of death, to guide our feet into the path of peace.

Luke 1:76-79

Christ is the Morning Star who, when the night of this world is past brings to His saints the promise of the light of life and opens everlasting day.

Venerable Bede

THE HEAD
OF THE CHURCH

And he is the head of the body,
the church; he is the beginning
and the firstborn from among
the dead, so that in everything
he might have the supremacy.

~ Colossians 1:18 ~

The Head of the Church

The head is the most important part of the body. It gives the body identity and direction. When we talk about Christ as the Head of the Church, we remember that He is the One who has authority over the Body and is to be obeyed in every way. He is our leader, our captain, our master.

Believers are placed in the Body of Christ by the Holy Spirit so that they will work in union under the authority and headship of Christ to do His will and bring glory to the Father.

The image of Christ as Head of the Church suggests His intimate relationship with each part of the body – with each believer – and His love and care for His body.

From His Word

Now I want you to realize that the head of every man is Christ, and the head of the woman is man, and the head of Christ is God.

1 Corinthians 11:3

And he made known to us the mystery of his will according to his good pleasure, which he purposed in Christ, to be put into effect when the times will have reached their fulfillment – to bring all things in heaven and on earth together under one head, even Christ.

Ephesians 1:9-10

And God placed all things under his feet and appointed him to be head over everything for the church, which is his body, the fullness of him who fills everything in every way.

Ephesians 1:22-23

I will also appoint him my firstborn, the most exalted of the kings of the earth.

Psalm 89:27

The Head of the Church

Instead, speaking the truth in love, we will in all things grow up into him who is the Head, that is, Christ.

Ephesians 4:15

According to his power that is at work within us, to him be glory in the church and in Christ Jesus throughout all generations, for ever and ever! Amen.

Ephesians 3:20-21

A Christian church is a body or collection of persons, voluntarily associated together, professing to believe what Christ teaches, to do what Christ enjoins, to imitate His example, cherish His Spirit, and make known His gospel to others.

Robert Fleming Sample

CORNERSTONE

Built on the foundation
of the apostles and prophets,
with Christ Jesus himself
as the chief cornerstone.

~ Ephesians 2:20 ~

Cornerstone

The Church is represented as a building that has been built on the foundation of the apostles and prophets and of which Jesus Christ is the cornerstone.

The cornerstone is important for ensuring that the walls join properly and that they are built straight.

When Jesus is our cornerstone, we can know that what we build in our lives will be straight and true and something that will be a worthy dwelling place for the King of heaven.

From His Word

For no one can lay any foundation other than the one already laid, which is Jesus Christ.

1 Corinthians 3:11

"Therefore everyone who hears these words of mine and puts them into practice is like a wise man who built his house on the rock. The rain came down, the streams rose, and the winds blew and beat against that house; yet it did not fall, because it had its foundation on the rock."

Matthew 7:24-25

For in Scripture it says: "See, I lay a stone in Zion, a chosen and precious cornerstone, and the one who trusts in him will never be put to shame."

1 Peter 2:6

So then, just as you received Christ Jesus as Lord, continue to live in him, rooted and built up in him, strengthened in the faith as you were taught, and overflowing with thankfulness.

Colossians 2:6-7

Cornerstone

And in him you too are being built together to become a dwelling in which God lives by his Spirit.

Ephesians 2:22

Now we know that if the earthly tent we live in is destroyed, we have a building from God, an eternal house in heaven, not built by human hands.

2 Corinthians 5:1

In him the whole building is joined together and rises to become a holy temple in the Lord.

Ephesians 2:21

> Let him who wants a true church cling to the Word by which everything is upheld.
>
> Martin Luther

FAITHFUL AND TRUE

I saw heaven standing open
and there before me
was a white horse,
whose rider is called
Faithful and True.
With justice he judges
and makes war.

~ Revelation 19:11 ~

Faithful and True

Central to the character of Christ is His total dependability. We can rely on Him fully, knowing that He will never let us down, never forsake us, never abandon us.

He does not change like shifting shadows. He is the solid and unshakeable rock on which we can find safety and security.

Christ is called Faithful and True, and because these qualities define His character, He is able to justly, fairly and righteously judge all mankind. We can depend on His love and mercy every day of our lives.

From His Word

Jesus Christ, who is the faithful witness, the first-born from the dead, and the ruler of the kings of the earth.

Revelation 1:5

Therefore God exalted him to the highest place and gave him the name that is above every name.

Philippians 2:9

These are the words of the Amen, the faithful and true witness, the ruler of God's creation.

Revelation 3:14

For this reason he had to be made like his brothers in every way, in order that he might become a merciful and faithful high priest in service to God, and that he might make atonement for the sins of the people.

Hebrews 2:17

Faithful and True

All the ways of the LORD are loving and faithful for those who keep the demands of his covenant.

Psalm 25:10

Give thanks to the LORD, for he is good. His love endures forever.

Psalm 136:1

For the love of God is broader
Than the measures of man's mind;
And the heart of the Eternal
Is most wonderfully kind.

F. W. Faber

Your Bridegroom

Let us rejoice and be glad
and give him glory!
For the wedding
of the Lamb has come,
and his bride
has made herself ready.

~ Revelation 19:7 ~

Your Bridegroom

Christ is the Bridegroom and the Church is the Bride. He lavishes His love and care on us, as a man does on his newly wed wife. The image of the Bridegroom is used throughout the Bible to help us understand the depth of the relationship God longs to have with us – intimate, loving and united through Christ.

When we realize that Christ is our spiritual husband, we begin to experience love beyond what we could ever think or imagine. It surpasses every human relationship we could ever know in intensity, purity and acceptance.

It is more satisfying and more fulfilling than anything on earth. The full and perfect love of God truly satisfies our deepest longings and meets our every need.

From His Word

Husbands, love your wives, just as Christ loved the church and gave himself up for her to make her holy, cleansing her by the washing with water through the word, and to present her to himself as a radiant church, without stain or wrinkle or any other blemish, but holy and blameless.

Ephesians 5:25-27

I saw the Holy City, the new Jerusalem, coming down out of heaven from God, prepared as a bride beautifully dressed for her husband.

Revelation 21:2

Jesus answered, "How can the guests of the bridegroom mourn while he is with them? The time will come when the bridegroom will be taken from them; then they will fast."

Matthew 9:15

"At midnight the cry rang out: 'Here's the bride-groom! Come out to meet him!'"

Matthew 25:6

Your Bridegroom

As a bridegroom rejoices over his bride, so will your God rejoice over you.

Isaiah 62:5

Then the angel said to me, "Write: 'Blessed are those who are invited to the wedding supper of the Lamb!'" And he added, "These are the true words of God."

Revelation 19:9

Is it a small thing in your eyes to be loved by God – to be the son, the spouse, the love, the delight of the King of glory? Christian, believe this and think about it: you will be eternally embraced in the arms of the love which was from everlasting and will extend to everlasting – of the love that brought the Son of God's love from heaven to earth.

Richard Baxter

KING OF KINGS AND LORD OF LORDS

On his robe and on his thigh
he has this name written:
KING OF KINGS
AND LORD OF LORDS.

~ Revelation 19:16 ~

King of kings and Lord of lords

One of the last titles that Christ is given in the Bible is the one that encompasses His greatness and victory. He is the King of kings and the Lord of lords.

At the end of time every knee will bow and every tongue confess that Jesus Christ is Lord. And He will establish His righteous rule over all the earth. We will see Him in the fullness of His radiance, glory and beauty.

His kingdom is an everlasting kingdom and His rule will have no end.

His sovereignty will be established forever and we will worship Him for His goodness, mercy and love forever.

From His Word

Above his head they placed the written charge against him: THIS IS JESUS, THE KING OF THE JEWS.

Matthew 27:37

Then he said, "Jesus, remember me when you come into your kingdom."

Luke 23:42

If you confess with your mouth, "Jesus is Lord," and believe in your heart that God raised him from the dead, you will be saved.

Romans 10:9

I charge you to keep this command without spot or blame until the appearing of our Lord Jesus Christ, which God will bring about in his own time – God, the blessed and only Ruler, the King of kings and Lord of lords.

1 Timothy 6:13-15

King of kings and Lord of lords

"I have installed my King on Zion, my holy hill."

Psalm 2:6

They will make war against the Lamb, but the Lamb will overcome them because he is Lord of lords and King of kings – and with him will be his called, chosen and faithful followers.

Revelation 17:14

Wherever God rules over the human heart as King, there is the kingdom of God established.

Paul W. Harrison

OTHER BOOKS
IN THIS RANGE

1-86920-061-6

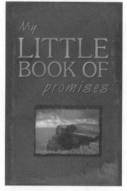

1-86920-062-4

1-86920-064-0

1-86920-063-2

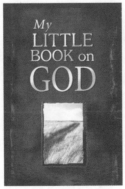

1-86920-540-5